Behavior Effectiveness Model (BEM)

Building Thriving Future
Using Behavior Effectiveness Model (BEM)

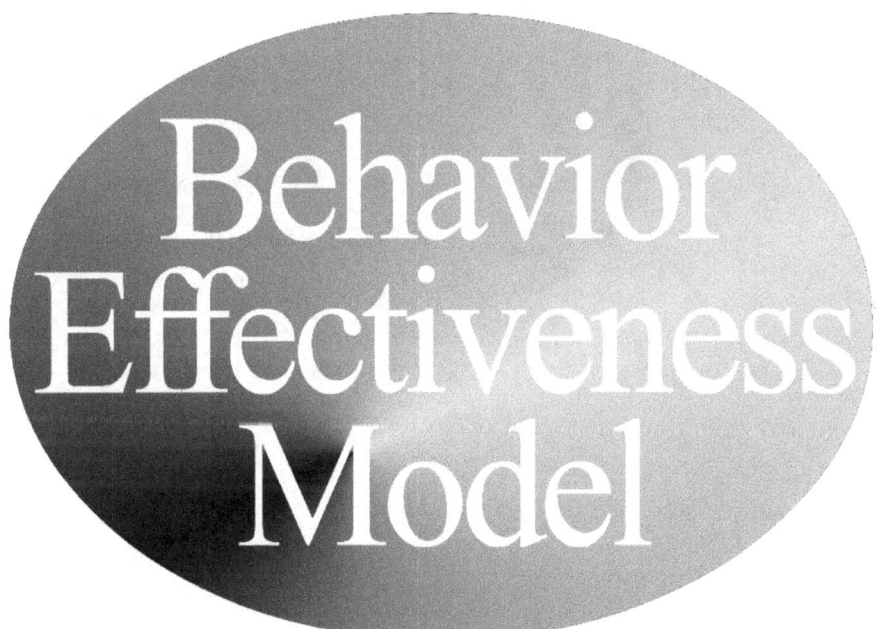

by

Gary "Chris" Christopherson
Former Senior Executive, U.S. Government
Founder, *Thrive!*® - Building a Thriving Future
Founder, HealthePeople® - Building a Healthy and Thriving Future

Nelson, WI   University Park, MD

ISBN-13: 978-1514758854
ISBN-10: 1514758857

DEDICATION

*People who help build, achieve and sustain
a surviving and thriving future for all forever.*

Dr. Patricia Haeuser, friend and supporter.

About The Author

Gary (Chris) Christopherson continues to work nationally and locally on improving health, reducing vulnerability and building a better future. Currently, he develops strategy, management and policy for creating, managing and sustaining large positive change and building a better and thriving future for all forever. ThrivingFuture.org He wrote the nonfiction books **Thrive! - Building a Thriving Future**, **Thrive! - People's Guide to a Thriving Future**, **Behavior Effectiveness Model (BEM)**, **The Thrive! Philosophy** and **Thrive! Endeavor** available via Amazon.com and ThriveEndeavor.org.

***Thrive!*®** (building a thriving future) draws on his 30+ years experience creating, managing and sustaining large positive change at national and local levels in public and private sectors. He founded **HealthePeople**® (building a healthy and thriving future; HealthePeople.com), ***via*Future** (creating large positive change) and **Vulnerable** (minimizing vulnerability). He served as a senior leader, manager and policymaker responsible for multi-billion dollar policy, programs and budgets and thousands of employees. His public service includes: Principal Deputy Assistant Secretary and Acting Assistant Secretary of Defense for Health Affairs and Senior Advisor, Department of Defense; Associate Director, Presidential Personnel, Executive Office of the President, White House; Senior Fellow, National Academy of Public Administration; Senior Advisor to Chief Operating Officer and Deputy Director for the Quality Improvement Group, Centers for Medicare and Medicaid Services, DHHS; Chief Information Officer, Veterans Health Administration and Senior Advisor to Under Secretary, Veterans Health Administration, VA; Senior Fellow and Scholar-In-Residence, Institute of Medicine, National Academy of Sciences; Director of Health Legislation, House Select Committee on Aging, U.S. House of Representatives.

He is a sculptor (GChris Sculpture) of abstract art, focusing on Thrive! sculptures and creating over 150 sculptures. See sculpture at GChris.com. He wrote science fiction novel **black box** and illustrated children's book **Angel, Thriving Creator of Artful Things**. Both are available via Amazon.com and GChris.com.

He received his bachelor's in political science and his master's in urban and regional planning from the University of Wisconsin – Madison, and did doctoral work in health policy and management at John Hopkins University School of Public Health.

Table of Contents

Summary
Behavior Effectiveness Model (BEM)

Much of the ineffectiveness of building a better and preferably thriving future can be traced to the inability and often lack of motivation to deal positively with human behavior. People can build a better future by learning to use behavioral skills and by using experience to increase effectiveness.

Building a better and thriving future, in part, can be measured in terms of human behavior. We need to better assist and/or affect decisions and actions and better design and evaluate change strategies in terms of behavior requirements. When we wish to understand, assist and/or affect the person's or persons' behavior in a specific decision or action or over a series of decisions or actions, we need a "handle" which identifies discrete determinants of behavior and provides a theory which indicates how these determinants affect near and long term behavior. A modified behavior theory, Expectancy Theory (E-T), provides insight in that respect.

The Behavior Effectiveness Model (BEM), an extension and refinement of E-T, assumes that behavior determinants can be identified for behavior objectives, and that we want more effective models and tools for achieving behavior objectives.[1]

The author developed, uses and recommends BEM as an effective model and tool for understanding and improving positive change efforts and building a better, thriving future for a person, for a community and for the world.

---

[1] In other publications, this is referred to as the Behavioral Effectiveness Model.

1. Behavior Effectiveness Models for Building Better Future.

Much of the ineffectiveness of building a better and preferably a thriving future can be traced to the inability and often lack of motivation to deal positively with human behavior. Traditionally, people trying to effect positive change (e.g., building a better and thriving future) are not sufficiently capable of or motivated toward dealing with human behavior. The author's purpose is to recommend that effective dealing with human behavior is a critical skill that can be acquired and is enhanced through extensive experience. People can build a better future by learning to use behavioral skills and by using experience to increase effectiveness.

Building a better and thriving future, in part, can be measured in terms of human behavior. For example, when we talk about user problems, we refer to the person's lack of ability or lack of motivation to do some thing. When a community wants to achieve some positive change and outcome, people must be able (e.g., have sufficient funding, have no legal restrictions, have requisite knowledge and skills) and motivated (e.g., see it as desirable, see it filling a need). For the community, implementers of change must be able and motivated to accept and execute the change. Implementers must see the change as effective in achieving personal and/or community outcomes. We need to better assist and/or affect decisions and actions and better design and evaluate change strategies in terms of behavior requirements.

When we wish to understand, assist and/or affect the person's or persons' behavior in a specific decision or action or over a series of decisions or actions, we need a "handle" which identifies discrete determinants of behavior and provides a theory which indicates how these determinants affect near and long term behavior. A modified behavior theory, Expectancy Theory (E-T), provides insight in that respect. For changing people's behavior to build a better future, the theory has face validity and substantial research (related to job performance and satisfaction) supporting different parts of the theory.

The Behavior Effectiveness Model (BEM), an extension and refinement of E-T, assumes that behavior determinants can be identified for behavior objectives, and that we want more effective models and tools for achieving behavior objectives.[2] If these are valid assumptions, then we need to identify and analyze alternative behavior models, review research and theory on decision-making and task performance, define and analyze the BEM approach, and evaluate BEM's possible application to positive change efforts, including personal, community, country and global efforts.

The author developed, uses and recommends BEM as an effective model and tool for understanding and improving positive change efforts and building a better, thriving future for a person, for a community and for the world.

---

[2] In other publications, this is referred to as the Behavioral Effectiveness Model.

2

2. Expectancy Theory Models as Foundations for Behavior Effectivness Model (BEM).

Alternative models, as precursors to the Behavior Effectiveness Model (BEM), have a history dating back five decades and grew out of theory and research on worker motivation and performance. That theory and research tries to explain a worker's performance on the job on a day-to-day basis over time. To apply the models' concepts, we assume that performance includes an initial decision to perform (behave) in a certain way and includes continuous or discrete decisions to continue or not continue performance (behavior) consistent with that initial decision depending on what happened after the initial decision.

A substantial body of theory has been written and empirical research carried out on a behavioral-cognitive theory called "expectancy theory" (E-T), "instrumentality theory", etc. The initial work on motivation and job performance was done by Victor Vroom (1964). (See Figure 2.1.) In his formulation, performance was a function of the interaction between a worker's force (or motivation) to perform and his ability. Force was a function of the valence (or value) of each performance level and the perceived probability that a certain amount of effort will lead to that performance level. The valence of each performance level is a function of the sum of the interactions between the valence of the second level outcomes (e.g., pay, recognition) and the probability that a performance level will lead to these second level outcomes. The person would choose the effort level with the strongest positive or weakest negative force.

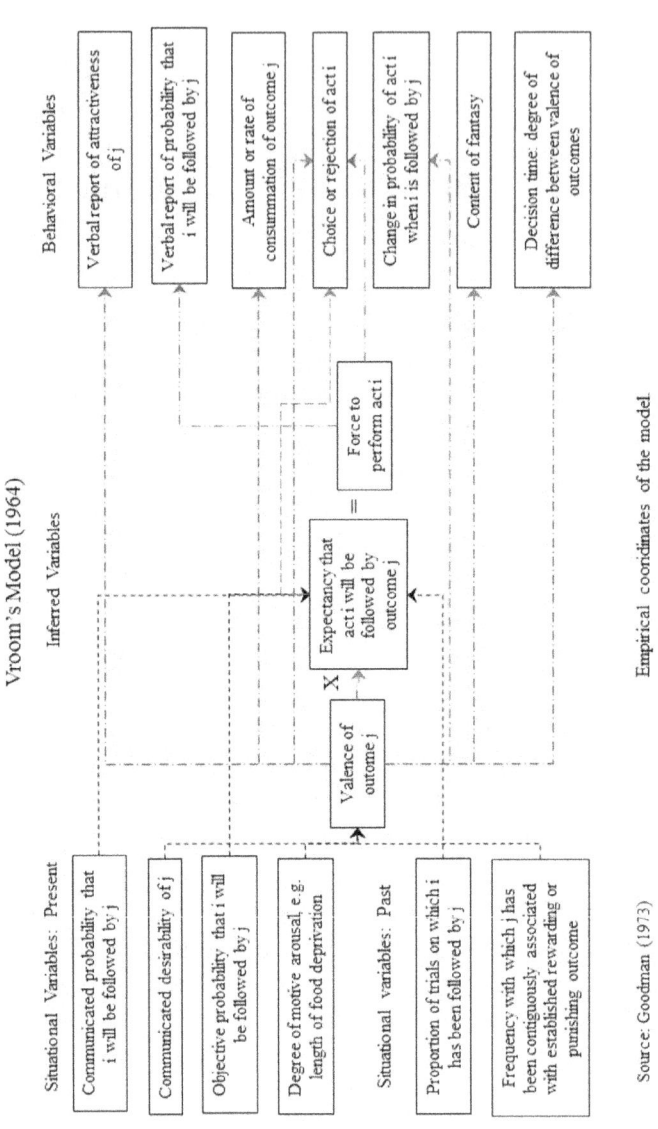

Figure 2.1. Vroom's Model (1964).

4

In 1968, Porter and Lawler revised Vroom's model. (See Figure 2.2.)

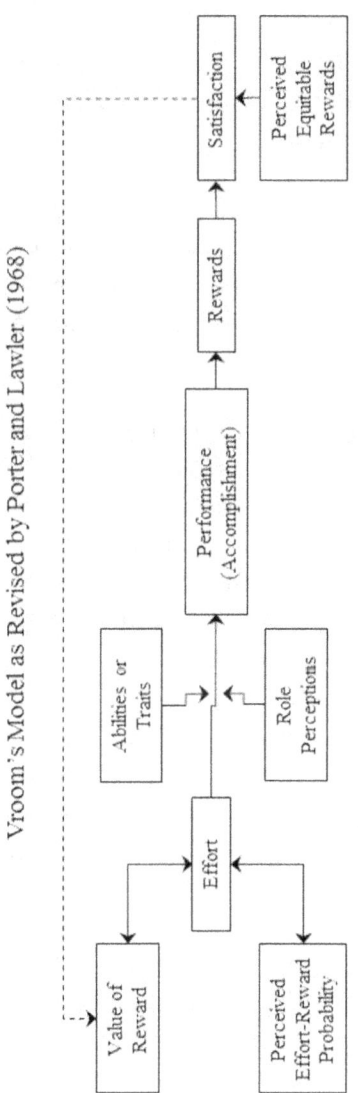

Figure 2.2. Vroom Model as Revised by Lawler and Porter.

They saw performance as function of effort, ability, and role perception. In addition, they added the concept of equity as a modifier of satisfaction. Otherwise, their model is fairly consistent with Vroom's model. Galbraith and Cummings (1967) made the distinction between intrinsic and extrinsic outcomes. Lawler (1971, 1973) updated and expanded the 1968 Porter and Lawler model. (See Figure 2.3.) In this revision, internal and external rewards (outcomes) are delineated, problem solving is added as a mediating factor, and past experience is introduced.

Goodman (1973) developed an organization learning model. (See Figure 2.4.). In his model, learning processes were added which included communication, generalization, and reinforcement. His model identifies antecedent factors (the individual, his/her role, the organization structure) as well.

Another model, a further refinement of the expectancy theory, was developed by Cummings and Schwab (1973). (See Figure 2.5.) Their model separates intrinsic and extrinsic outcomes, separates first and second level outcomes, separates individual from organizational variables, indicates where organizational variables can have effect, and presents a dynamic, interactive process between the organization and the individual. The Cummings and Schwab and Cummings models' (like BEM) variables include:

1) independent variables: organizational and environmental variables, ability, motivation, intrinsic and extrinsic rewards (or consequences) and expectancies, and

2) dependent variables: performance (behavior, decisions) and satisfaction (attitudes).

Cummings (1973) made further refinements on their model. (See Figure 2.6.) In this refinement, Cummings included an interactive effect between ability and motivation, defined expectancies I, II and III, and included voluntary withdrawal behaviors growing out of dissatisfaction. Organizational variables and feedback loops are not in the diagram but are implied and will be described later.

6

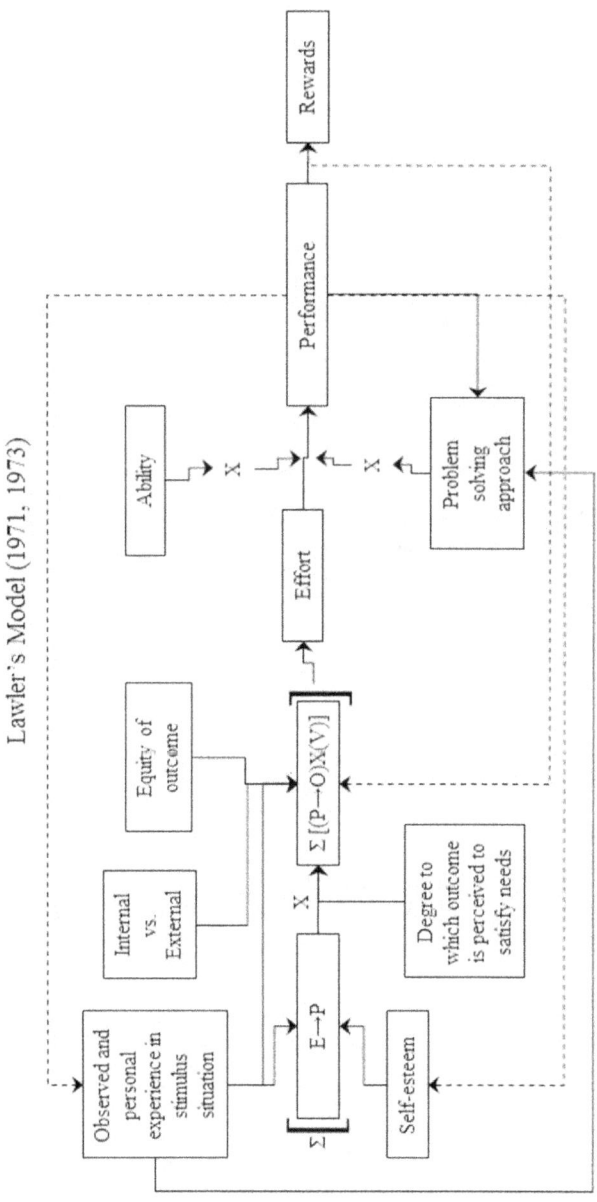

Figure 2.3. Lawler Model (1971)

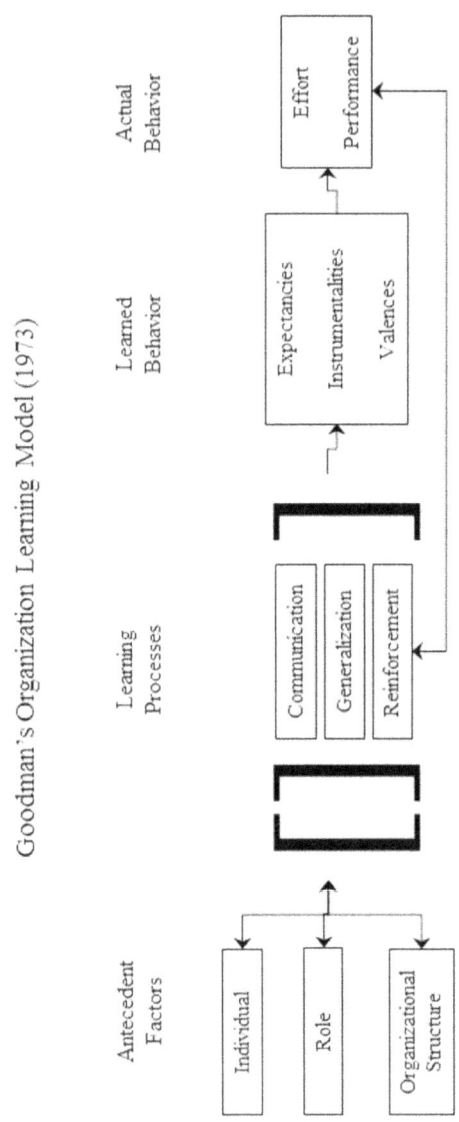

Goodman's Organization Learning Model (1973)

| Antecedent Factors | Learning Processes | Learned Behavior | Actual Behavior |

Individual

Role

Organizational Structure

Communication

Generalization

Reinforcement

Expectancies
Instrumentalities
Valences

Effort
Performance

Figure 2.4. Goodman Model (1973)

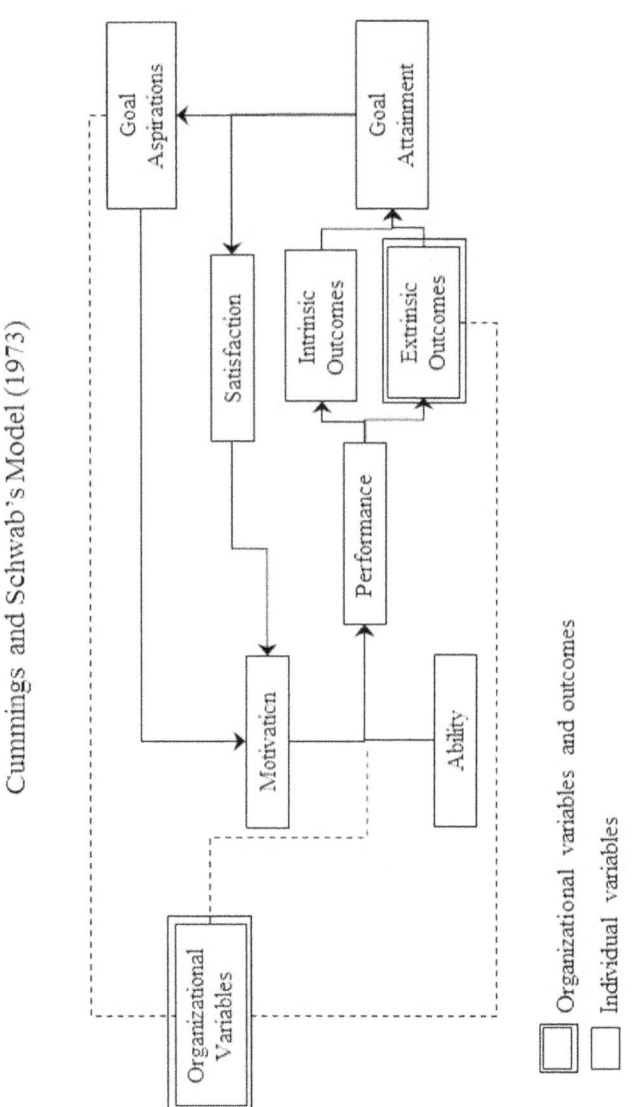

Cummings and Schwab's Model (1973)

Figure 2.5. Cummings and Schwab Model (1973)

9

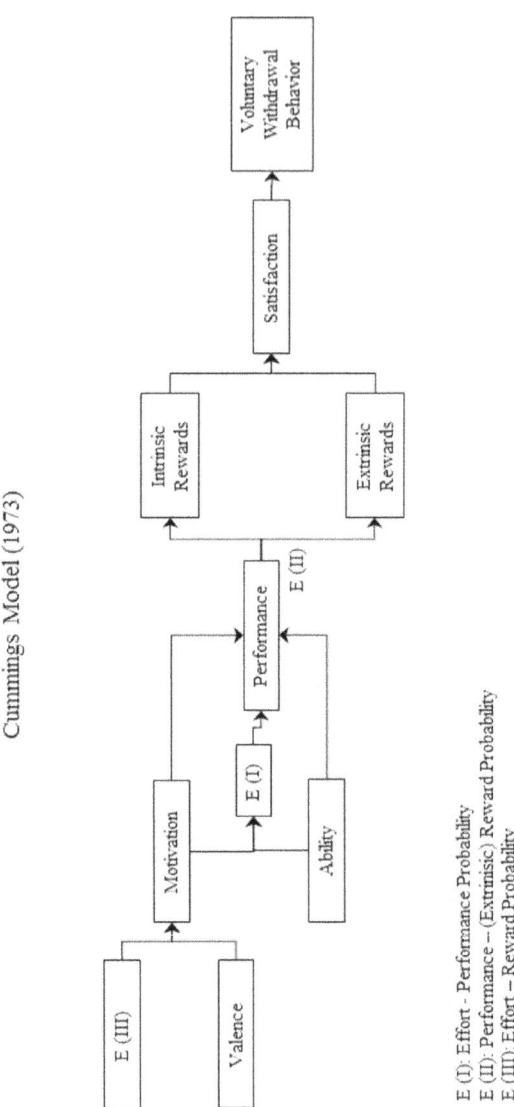

Cummings Model (1973)

E (I): Effort - Performance Probability
E (II): Performance – (Extrinsic) Reward Probability
E (III): Effort – Reward Probability

Figure 2.6. Cummings Model (1973)

The following table identifies, defines, indicates measures or rates, and provides comment on both independent and dependent variables. (See Table 2.1)

Table 2.1 Expectancy Theory Variables			
Variable	Define	Research Definition	Comments
Expectancy I	whether or not the individal expects to accomplish first level outcomes	the subject's probability estimate that his/her effort will lead to first level outcomes (House, Shapiro, Wahba, 1973)	some support for when tested
Expectancy II	whether or not achievement of first level outcomes are expected to be instrumental in the attainment of second level outcomes	the subject's probability estimate that first level outcomes will lead to extrinsic rewards (House, Shapiro, Wahba, 1973)	some support for EII when tested alone
Expectancy III	whether or not the individual expects to attain second level outcomes	the subject's probability estimate that his/her effort will lead to intrinsic and extrinsic rewards (Cummings, 1971)	limited support for combining EI and EII motivation
Valence	the value which an individual places on the consequences of his behavior	intrinsic and extrinsic valences (Galbraith & Cummings, 1967)	the value placed on instrinsic consequences may be as strong or stronger than extrinsic consequences
Ability	an individual's current capacity to perform some task or tasks	individual characteristics including various types of intellectual factors such as verbal, numerical, spatial skills and the like. also included are manual factors, strengths, dexterities as well as personality traits (Cummings & Schwab, 1973)	generally relates only to the individual's ability not to environmental factors (resources and other people's skills) which affect the individual's ability

Organizational Variables	those variables which are within the organization's power to materially influence	task design, management behavior, reward and punishment systems, organization structure (Cummings & Schwab, 1973)	results do not seem consistent; suggest depends on the individual worker; do not adequately account for complexity of human behavior of either leader or subordinate
First Level Outcomes	job behavior; outcome of an individual's efforts with respect to task performance or accomplishment	performance (Porter & Lawler, 1968), work goal accomplishment (House, 1971)	difficult to measure for many jobs
Second Level Outcomes	consequences to which first level outcomes are expected to lead	reward and punishment (Cummings & Schwab, 1973), intrinsic reward/ punishments which are self-administered	rewards must be tied to high performance to be effective; need to look more at more than money
Satisfaction	an individual's attitude toward his/her performance, outcomes, organizational variables	measures of attitude toward work, pay, co-workers, supervision, promotion (Job Description Index)	difficult to measure; some question whether refers to attitude, need deprivation or both

In a House, Shapiro, and Wahba (1973) review of Expectancy Theory, the changes since Vroom's model were identified:
1) a distinction between first and second level outcomes,
2) identification of intrinsic rewards,
3) the distinction between expectancy I and expectancy II, and
4) elaboration to predict the effect of additional variables.

In addition, they summarized research results as follows:

1) The findings of the thirty-one studies are not always consistent and at times are contradictory.

2) It appears that support for the theory is still weak – the variances explained by the various parts of the theory are usually rather low.

3) It is not clear which is the best combination of variables that provides the best predictor or predictors of effort and/or performance and satisfaction. What is clear is that the individual components are less predictive than the aggregate model.

4) The most important single predictor variable seems to be EII, particularly for predicting job satisfaction. It does also exhibit some strength in predicting effort and/or performance.

5) The intrinsic and extrinsic valences as predictors show mixed results. It is probably true that an employee values intrinsic rewards more highly than extrinsic rewards because he/she does not have to depend upon others for them. In turn, however, intrinsic rewards that lead to job satisfaction do not necessarily have to result in job effort or job performance.

6) The most significant conclusion reached is that the theory has definite boundary conditions such as perceived contingency of pay being dependent upon performance in addition to the boundaries formed by ability, organization structure and climate, and individual differences.

Finally, House, Shapiro, and Wahba indicated problems which need to be solved:

1) As it stands, expectancy theory still implicity makes rationality assumptions underlying choice behavior, in particular the assumed preferences and indifferences; the independence of relevant outcomes; and the independence of expectancy of outcomes.

2) The choice of criterion, embodied in the current formulation of the theory is based upond the concept of maximization.

Alternative criteria such as "satisfying" and the "sure principal" should be considered.

3) A fuller explication of the boundary conditions associated with the work situation is required, particularly, the contingencies of rewards without which the theory becomes non-operative.

4) There are a number of measurement issues that need to be discussed, in particular the lack of standard measures of both expectancy and valence and the criterion against which the theory is validated.

5) As yet, few studies have considered negative valences and successfully developed a measure of an instrumentality independent from expectancy.

6) Most of the studies have utilized a cross group analysis while the theory is an individual theory, evidently there is a need for within individual analysis.

7) Schmidt (1973) states that E and V are typically measured using scales lacking a rational zero point and are best interval in nature. He claims that multiplication of such scales, as proposed in VIE theory, are theoretically not a meaningful operation.

Though E-T seems to have conceptual (face) validity, we should be cautious about application. We need to be more cognizant of the individualistic implication of the theory when we try to apply the theory to groups or classes of individuals. The research has been somewhat inconclusive but support seems to depend on the conditions, assumptions made, test population, the number of independent variables, and which parts and how many parts of the theory were tested.

3. What Behavior Effectiveness Model (BEM) is.

The Behavior Effectiveness Model (BEM) is built upon several related models including expectancy theory, instrumentality theory, theory of reasoned action, contingency theory, system theory, social cognitive theory, and behavioral theory. BEM has been in use and refined over 30-40 years by the author.

The first version of this model was called the Behavioral Effectiveness Model (BEM) and was created as part of the author's Master's Theses entitled <u>People Planning: Increasing Planning Effectiveness by Working with User and Implementer Behavior</u>.[3] Over the past several decades, the model has gone through a number of refinements based on the author's extensive career as a senior executive in public policy and public administration at the local and national levels. (See "About the Author".)

In the previous chapter, the discussion focused on Expectancy Theory (E-T) in relation to task performance and satisfaction. In terms of the basic interrelationships, the Behavior Effectiveness Model (BEM) is similar to E-T, but differs in the content of its terms (e.g., decision and action behavior as a first level outcome instead of just task performance), the application environment (e.g., a whole person, a whole community and the whole world instead of just a structured organization), and the role it plays in that environment (e.g., assisting and/or affecting behavior from the persons and/or change agents point of view). In order to be useful for the person and/or change agents, the theory needs to focus primarily on decision and action behavior.

---

[3] Department of Urban and Regional Planning, University of Wisconsin – Madison, 1974.

To achieve that focus, variables need to be defined for BEM. The following table examines these variables. (See Table 3.1)

Table 3.1 Behavior Effectiveness Theory (BEM) Variables			
Variable	Define	Measure	Related Questions
Valence (Intrinsic & Extrinsic)	For each alternative behavior, the person sums up the positive and negative values for each perceived consequence of an alternative and then sums the value for all the perceived consequences of an alternative.	If the perceived consequences of doing alternative A are perceived as a 10% loss of votes in the next election, $1 million in campaign contributions, better schools for the person's children, increased respect of friends and fellow elected officials and the person feels a sense of accomplishment, the person might rank those consequences from most desirable to most undesirable and rate them form -100 to 100.	How much does the person want or not want the consequences of alternative A?
Effort to consequences relationship	For each alternative behavior, the person estimates the probability that the person's efforts will lead to a set of consequences.	For each of the above consequences, the person may estimate a .5 probability that each of the first three will occur and a .9 probability that the rest will occur as a result of the person's efforts.	How likely/unlikely that the person's efforts to do alternative A will lead to each of the perceived consequences?

Motivation	The amount of effort which the person is willing to expend and in what direction.	Multiply each consequence's valence times the probability of its occurrence, sum these products for all the consequences of alternative A, and compare to any other alternatives.	How much effort is the person likely to expend and in what direction?
Ability	The person estimates the probability that if the person tries (expends effort), the person will be able to make a decision or take action.	For each alternative, the person may estimate the probability that if the person tries, the person will succeed at making a decision or taking action.	Does the person have or perceive that the person has the ability to do alternative A?
Behavior (Decision, Action)	The person's making a decision or taking action.	The likelihood that the person will do some thing (behave or decide in a certain way) is dependent on the person's ability and motivation to do do that something and is moderated by the person's perceptions of 1. the probability that if the person tries, the person will succeed, and 2. the probability that the person's success will lead to satisfactory consequences.	What does the person want to do and/or what do we want the person to do?
Consequences	The results form the person's making a decision or taking action.	The person lists all the perceived consequences of the person's expected behavior.	What are the consequences of doing alternative A?

Effort to behavior relationship	The person estimates the probability that if the person tries (expends effort), the person will be able to make a decision or take action.	For each alternative, the person may estimate the probability that if the person tries, the person will succeed at making a decision or taking action.	How likely/unlikely that if the person tries to do alternative A, the person will succeed?
Behavior to consequences relationship	For each alternative behavior, the person estimates the probability that if the person behaves in a certain way, conseqences will result.	For each alternative, the person may estimate the probability (0.0 to 1.0) that if the person behaves in a certain way (performs a task or makes a decision) that certain consequences will result. For example, by doing A, the probability might be .5 that the perceived consequences would result	How likely/unlikely that doing alternative A will lead to each of the perceived consequences?
Satisfaction (Acceptance)	The person's attitude and subsequent behavior resulting from the actual consequences of a certain behavior.	After doing alternative A and the consequences result, if the person says the person is satisfied and the effect on subsequent behavior is consistent with that statement, we conclude to the best of our knowledge that the person is satisfied. Behavioral indicators include verbal expressions, on-task behavior, and response to similar future decisions.	Is the person satisfied with the consequences of alternative A? How does the person behave subsequently?

Broadening Cummings (1973) model to include decisions, actions and other behavior outside of a structured organization, the resulting model suggests a way to look at change efforts in terms of meeting behavioral objective and facilitating decision-making. BEM is concerned with increasing the effectiveness of those behavioral processes in two contexts – planning and implementing positive change, e.g., building a better and thriving future. (See Figure 3.1)

BEM hypothesizes that when people behave (decide and/or take action) in certain ways, their behavior can be better understood by looking at the independent variables which affect the dependent variables – behavior (decision, action) and attitudes (satisfaction, acceptance). For example, BEM indicates that when people are motivated (e.g., they try hard to decide and/or take action) their success or effectiveness at doing some thing depends on ability as well. The converse (i.e., when people are able, they need to be motivated) holds as well. In addition, though people's short run behavior may be determined by how they perceive the situation, in the long run the objective realities (e.g., getting / not getting equitable rewards, ability/inability to meet high expectations) will affect motivation and behavior.

Behavior Effectiveness Model (BEM)

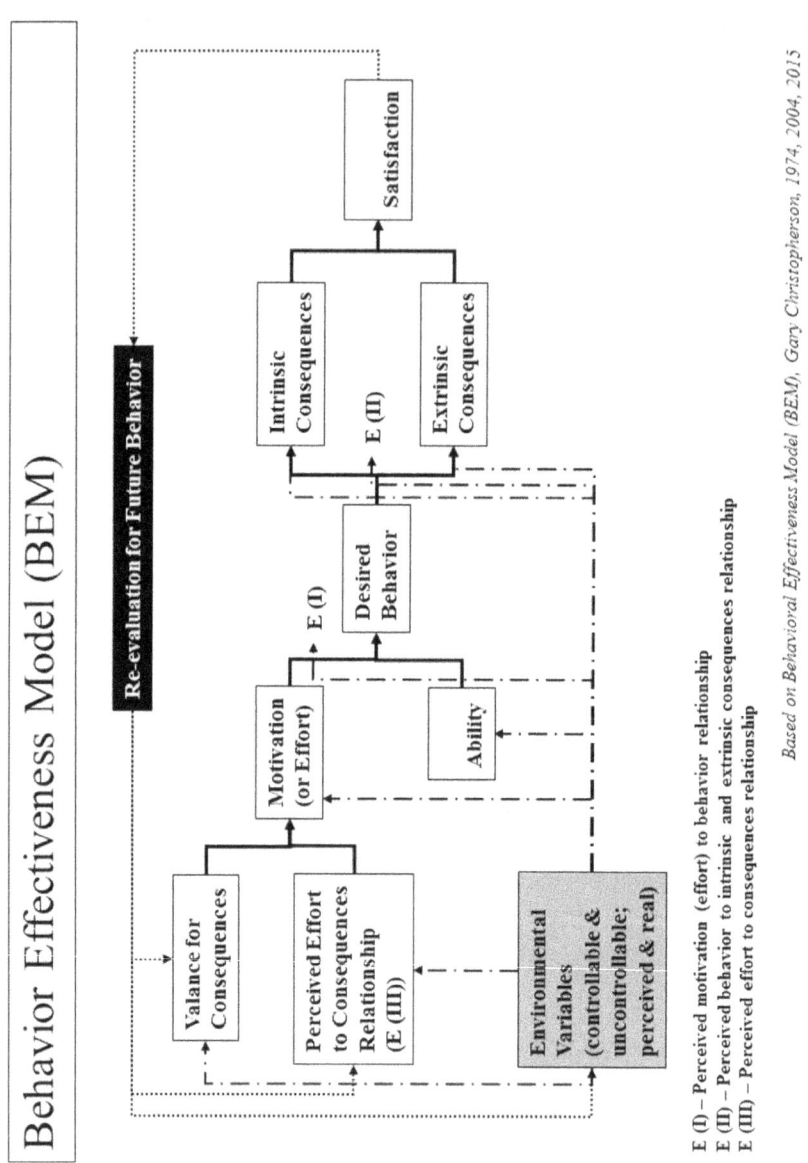

Figure 3.1. Behavior Effectiveness Model (BEM) (Christopherson, 1974, 2015).

At this point, a few statements of assumptions and/or principles are needed to further clarify BEM's requirements and limitations.

1. Though studies use E-T to explain behavior and the factors which determine that behavior, inclusiveness of research results limits E-T utility. BEM is used as a conceptual framework which indicates ways of facilitating, evaluating behavior and its determinants.

2. BEM's effectiveness is somewhat proportional to the accuracy and completeness of our information on the person(s).

3. A distinction needs to be made between what the person(s) intends or tries to do and what the person(s) actually will do.

4. To the extent feasible, each variable should be approporiately weighted for determining behavior.

5. Ideally, BEM works best for individual persons. However, BEM can be used for multiple persons who have common enough characteristics so as to be treated similarly. We need to be very wary of making this latter assumption and to have a mechanism to handle exceptions.

6. For each use of BEM, it is better to use multiple measures where feasible.

7. When obtaining information directly from the person(s), a) ask the person(s) to generate an initial list (e.g., of rewards), b) add the controllable environmental variables to the person(s) list, and c) then ask for a ranking and/or rating of value of probability and value.

8. BEM explains behavior in terms of optimal outcomes and/or satisficing outcomes.

9. When behavior changes are large and difficult, very strong positive and/or negative reinforcers may be needed or the changes might be accomplished incrementally over time using less powerful reinforcers.

10. Decision (and action) behavior may be either discrete (the conscious and deliberate making of a decision) or continuous (a series of behaviors over time which are consistent with the initial decision and are not consciously re-evaluated).

Decision choice may be either discrete (a conscious choice among a limited number of alternatives or along a range).

11. When applying BEM, the option is usually open to modify the person's (or persons') behavior and or the environment.

12. Distinctions need to be drawn between a) influencing the person's (or persons') behavior toward the person's (or persons') objectives, b) influencing the person's (or persons') behavior toward "community" objectives, and c) influencing the person's (or persons') behavior toward an organization's organizational objectives or another person's personal objectives.

13. Environmental variables can affect the number of variables which the person(s) might consider, the value placed on extrinsic outcomes or consequences, and the probabilities of each expectancy. For example, we might clarify (or, when appropriate, obscure) the variables, values and probabilities which affect the person's decision behavior. Or we might add/remove positive and/or negative consequences.

14. Program effectiveness can be measured by criteria of fit to individualistic assumptions, program quality for solving user problems or achieving user purposes, and program implementability in terms of acceptance and support by adopters and administrators. For example, to meet different personal or group needs, we might design multiple program components which deal with the different needs of different persons or sub-populations.

BEM can be applied to real world situations as follows. A target population is identified. That population is broken down into subgroups. These subgroups must have similar characteristics in terms of:

- ability,
- likely consequences or rewards and how much they are wanted,
- level of motivation, and

- how they perceive the relationships between their effort level, their actual behavior and expected level of satisfaction.

Ability can be measured in terms of resources (person-hours, money, legal power, informal power or influence, number of people, organization, equipment, control over natural resources, information, access to people, technology, formal (organizational) power, and resource utilization skills (inter-personal, organizing, managing, political, planning, analysis, technical).

Motivation (effort) is a product of how strongly certain expected consequences are wanted / not wanted and the perceived likelihood that efforts will lead to those expected consequences.

Actual behavior has both quality and quantity dimensions. Behavior acceptability can be judged from among alternatives and/or along a range of behavior. Behavior could be an initial behavior (a single decision and/or action) or behavior over time (multiple decisions and/or actions).

Consequences can be those administered by the environment (e.g., moncy, power, recognition, goods, services, security, religious sanction or support, feedback, sex, social interaction, control over future, important activities) or those self-administered (e.g., moral fit, use of valued skills, achievement of personal goal, personal pride, autonomy, identity). These consequences can be desirable/undesirable, presented/removed, in different amounts, on different schedules of administration, and/or vary in their effect for each person.

If we want to facilitate/affect behavior, then we should affect the determinants (or the perception of the determinants) of that behavior.

Any items which are on the ability list can be used to affect behavior by removing/adding and/or increasing/decreasing ability.

Motivation can be affected by adding/removing and/or increasing/decreasing the expected consequences, by a) changing the valence of consequences through peer, expert, "undesirables", media and/or notables influence, b) using the person's own list of desirable/undesirable consequences, adding on items we have control over and having the person rank and/or rate the listed consequences, and c) clarifying (or, when appropriate, obscuring) the relationship between the person's effort and the expected consequences.

Certain behaviors can be increased by adding more desirable consequences, removing undesirable consequences, and/or reducing the strength and frequency of undesirable consequences. To be effective, affecting the determinants must be contingent upon only acceptable behavior (or stopping unacceptable behavior). To reduce the likelihood of unacceptable behavior, we reverse the affecting of determinants to make the unacceptable behavior tied to undesirable/neutral consequences.

When the person perceives the probability that the person's efforts will lead to effective/ineffective behavior, the probability that the person's effective behavior will lead to desirable/undesirable consequences, and the probability that the person's efforts will lead to desirable/undesirable consequences, the person's probability perceptions may be influenced by clarifying (or when appropriate, obscuring)
- those relationships (e.g, the probabilities),
- the time lag between effort and consequences, effort and effective behavior, and effective behavior and consequences, and
- the ratio of effort/performance, performance/consequences, and effort/consequences).

If the expected behavior is unacceptable, then that behavior should be reduced/extinguished and an alternative acceptable behavior should be reinforced and supported.

4. What Behavior Effectiveness Model (BEM) does.

The Behavior Effectivenesss Model's (BEM) value lies in 1) being relatively parsimonious, 2) incorporating key aspects of other behavioral models, 3) being "computable" (i.e., it can use databases (personal and environmental characteristics, desired behaviors and tailored interventions)), 4) tailoring applicability to more than one person simultaneously by using individual characteristics and desired behavior(s) and 5) using evidence-based interventions that can be tailored to those characteristics and the desired behavior.

How does it work? As shown in Table 4.1, BEM is designed to 1) apply interventions that help achieve the desired target behavior, 2) learn more about the person or population involved, 3) learn more about interventions and 4) learn more about the "system" in which intervention are used. It can also be used for prediction, analysis and program development and evaluation. The model can be applied to 1) an individual person, 2) populations whose characteristics are sufficiently the same, and/or 3) populations of individuals for which each individual gets a personalized and tailored intervention. The model can be linked to a database so that it can use and produce information and support personalized and tailored interventions:
- For any number of individuals and over any period of time
- For one-time behaviors and behavior over time
- For change in a single behavior and multiple behaviors.

Table 4.1. "Behavior Effectiveness Model (BEM)" – Improving Personal Behavior/Performance

BEM use for achieving desired behavior is as follows:
1. Identify the person or population whose behavior is targeted.
2. Decide what is the desired behavior or behaviors. Note that some behavior is one-time and some is recurring.
3. Assess motivation in terms of its current and future characteristics.
4. Assess ability in terms of its current and future characteristics.
5. Assess environmental variables, both controllable and uncontrollable and both perceived and real.
6. Assess how motivation, ability and environmental variables are likely to affect future behavior without further intervention.
7. Assess what are likely to be the intrinsic (internal to the person or population) and extrinsic (external to the person or population) consequences of projected behavior and what is likely to be the person or population's satisfaction.
8. Assess how consequences and satisfaction are likely to affect future behavior
9. Assess how projected behavior, without further intervention, matches to desired behavior.
10. Assess what interventions will best move projected behavior to desired behavior for the near and long term.
11. Apply the interventions and assess their effect.
12. Adjust the interventions as needed over time and based on result.
13. Feed the interventions into overall strategy and supporting strategies.

As shown again in Figure 4.1 and in more detail in the spreadsheet in Figure 4.2, BEM has several elements that operate as inputs to or outputs from the intervention models used and help change behavior. The elements include the following:

1) Valence (value) of consequences is how the person(s) values the consequences that the person may or will face. They may be intrinsic (internal to person(s)) or extrinsic (external to person(s)).

2) Expectancy III (E (III)) is the person's or persons'perception (or the actual projected) probability that the person's or persons' effort will result in each consequence.

3) Motivation (effort) is what the person(s) is expected to try to do (that is, try to do the behavior) and is calculated using the "valence of consequences" and E (III) above.

4) Ability is the person's or persons' capability to do the behavior. Any ability that is essential to the behavior and is at low levels means that the person(s) is unlikely to be able to do the behavior even if other less essential ability factors are high.

5) Behavior is the desired behavior to achieve the desired vulnerability/thriving outcome. Behavior probability is calculated using motivation and ability probabilities.

6) Consequences are the expected results of effort to do the behavior or the behavior itself. Valence is modified to reflect the actual valence when the consequence occurred.

7) Expectancy I (E (I)) is the person's or persons' perception (or the actual projected) probability that the person's or persons' effort will result in desired behavior.

8) Expectancy II (E (II)) is the person's or persons' perception (or the actual projected) probability that the person's or pesons'behavior will result in intrinsic and/or extrinsic consequences.

9) Satisfaction is the person's or persons'level and direction (positive/negative) of satisfaction with what happens, especially as compared to expectations. It is especially

key when the behavior is recurring or when a future behavior is related.

10) Environmental factors (EF) are those outside influences affecting motivation and ability and may be current or projected. They include program interventions to improve probability of desired behavior initially and over time. They may be controllable or uncontrollable and may be real and/or perceived. They are factors outside the factors in the model. Environmental factors can impact the model at several points as noted by the "EF" arrows depicted in the model figure above.

There are several outputs provided by the model that predict what will happen initially and over time, including:

- Ability -- Given the person's or persons' own abilities and the impacting environmental factors (factors that negatively and/or positively impact the person's or persons' ability), how able is the person(s) to do the desired behavior?

- Motivation -- Given how the potential consequences are valued and how effort is expected to result in consequences, what is motivation direction/level?

- Behavior -- Given motivation, ability, consequences and expectations, what is the expected behavior, its likelihood, its intensity, and its direction?

- "Pre" Satisfaction -- Given expectations, motivation, ability, behavior and consequences, what is the expected satisfaction?

- "Post" Satisfaction -- Given what behavior and consequences actually happened, what is the actual satisfaction and what is its implication for subsequent behavior?

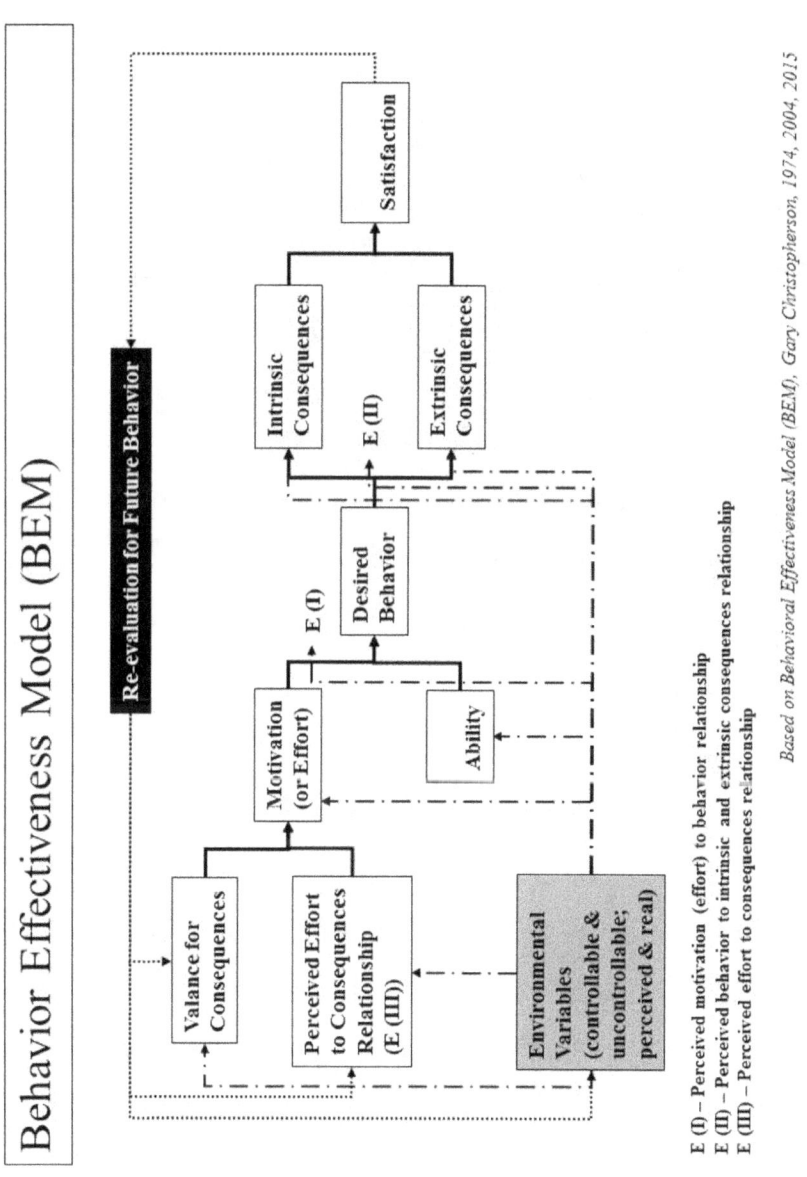

Figure 4.1. Behavior Effectiveness Model (BEM) (Christopherson, 1974, 2015).

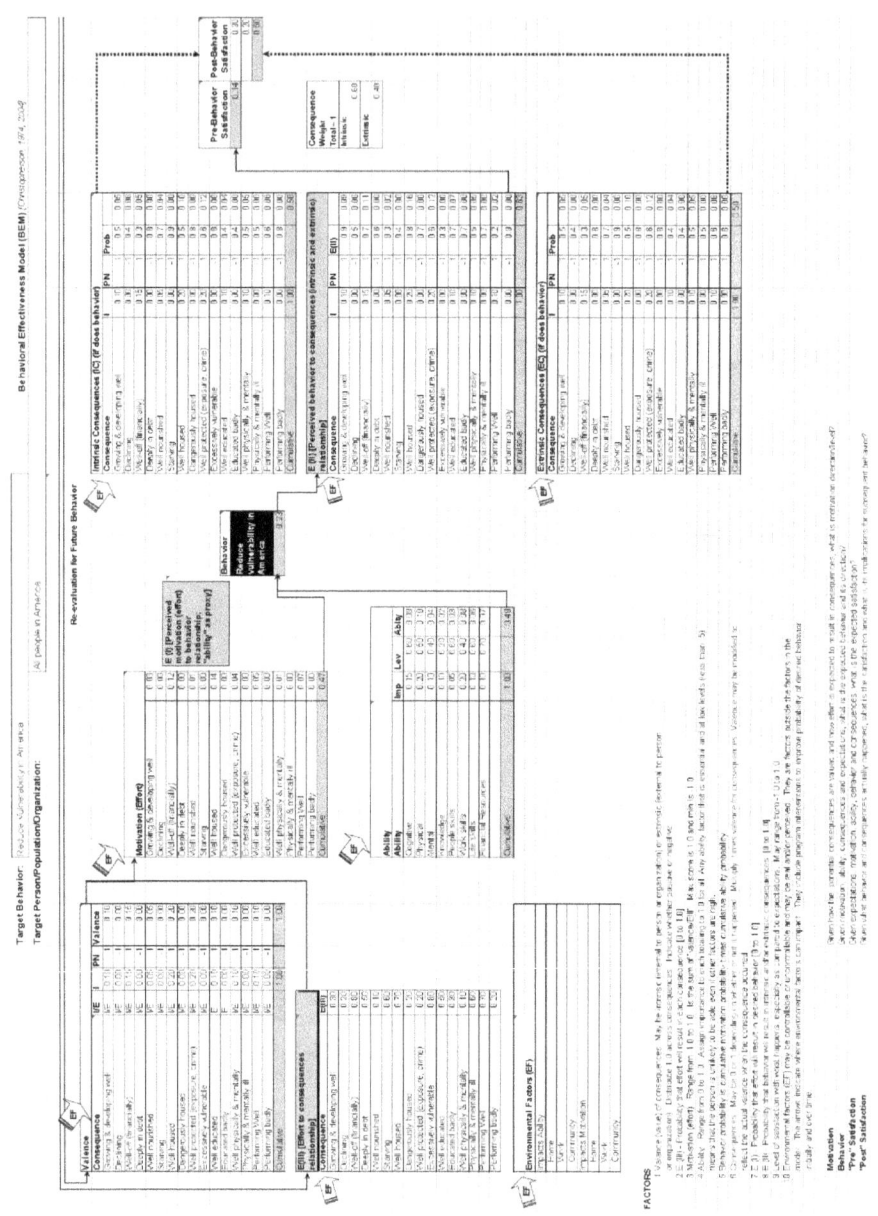

Figure 4.2. BEM Applied to Reducing Vulnerability in America and Beyond. (Christopherson, 2015)

BEM, as noted below, is designed and used here to 1) apply interventions that help achieve the desired target behavior, 2) learn more about the person(s) involved, 3) learn more about the intervention itself and 4) learn more about the "system" in which the intervention is used. Examples of the potential uses include:

- Impact behavior
  - Analyze current behavior and the factors that impact that behavior
  - Predict future behavior and the factors that impact that behavior
  - Support interventions that impact behavior and incorporate the factors that impact behavior
- Learn more about the person(s).
  - Information on ability and motivation.
  - Information that was initially incomplete or inaccurate.
  - Information that changes over time due to changes from the intervention, from the environment independently, and/or from the person independently.
- Learn more about the intervention.
  - On what individual person(s) does the intervention work and not work and what degrees in between (works X% of the time; produces Y% of the desired result)?
  - How can the intervention best be targeted for use by/with different individual persons?
  - How does the intervention need to be changed to match changes in individual persons?
  - How can the intervention be improved generally and for individual persons based on lessons learned?
- Learn more about the system in which the model is being used and the environment in which it and its persons operate.

BEM can be and is used here used for prediction, analysis and program development, including:

- It can be used and is used here as a predictive model for motivation/effort, behavior and satisfaction.
  - o The person's or persons' characteristics (valence or value of potential consequences; expectations that effort will lead to specific consequences; cognitive and physical ability) are entered into the model and predicted results (expected level of motivation/ effort, expected behavior and expected level of satisfaction) are processed through the model.
  - o The model also can utilize environmental factors that influence any the person's or persons' characteristics. The model also can then use the predicted results and environmental factors to predict subsequent effort, behavior and satisfaction.
- It can be used and is used here as an analytic model to better understand what is working and not working, why, and what changes are needed.
  - o If there is a lack of motivation, the model can help work through the perceived consequences, the perceived linkages of effort to those consequences and provide options for what needs to be changed.
  - o If the desired behavior is not occurring, the model helps work through what factors (e.g., persons' or persons' ability, their expectations about consequences, their general motivation, their satisfaction with previous efforts with an intervention, the effects of environmental factors) need to be changed.
  - o If the desired satisfaction is not achieved, the model can help work through why not and provide options for what needs to be changed.
- It can be used and is used here for program development to develop or modify a program intervention for particular individuals and/or generally.

o Based on the person's or persons' characteristics and the desired behavior, the program intervention can be designed or modified to improve likelihood of successfully achieving the desired behavior. For some persons, the focus might be on ability, motivation or both.

The model can be applied and is applied here to 1) an individual, 2) persons or populations whose characteristics are sufficiently the same, and/or 3) persons or populations of individuals for which each individual gets a personalized/customized/tailored intervention.

The model can be linked to a database so that it can produce information and support personalized/customized/tailored interventions:

- For any number of persons and over any period of time
- For one-time behaviors and behavior over time
- For change in a single behavior and multiple behaviors.

Figure 4.2 provides an example of how BEM works when applied to an issue such as reducing vulnerability and increasing thriving. The example is a relatively simple one that is applicable to either a person, persons or a population with very similar characteristics. It shows how the basic calculations would be done and what the results, would be on a first run of the model. To fully use the model, it should be run multiple times to see what changes occur and need to be incorporated into the model. For some uses, this basic model or even a simpler version may be adequate. For some uses, the model may need many more factors. It may need to be run separately for other persons or populations. If the target behavior is a recurring behavior, then the model should be rerun consistent with the recurring behavior and over the relevant time.

As is true for almost any model and as has been true over the past decades, BEM will improve with more use and the knowledge gained from that use.

How has it been used and helped? BEM's primary use to date has been for improving health. Its potential use is being explored in creating an overall strategy for reducing vulnerability and improving the status of a person, a non-geographic population, a community, a country or a broader area.

Its earliest use was in the middle 1970's, helping develop a high blood pressure control program in Milwaukee, Wisconsin. The desired behavior was adherence to methods for controlling high blood pressure. These methods could be medication use and/or life style change (e.g., diet, exercise, stress reduction). Through the use of BEM, the program was better able to get people to get their blood pressures checked and controlled and to determine the likely success of particular methods with a specific person and with persons with similar characteristics. The blood pressure control program was seen as a national model for community blood pressure control.

BEM is also being used on the cross-cutting issue of vulnerability. Here it is being used to help identify what behaviors are associated with vulnerability and thriving. It helps identify what ability and motivational factors are and would be determinants of vulnerability and thriving behavior as well as establishing what interventions to use to reduce such vulnerability and maximize thriving. Based on these, the potential strategy, **Vulnerable In America and World**, was created for minimizing vulnerability and maximizing thriving for a whole population, in this case America as a whole. As indicated earlier, the overall strategy has not been used to date, but is ready for application.

With respect to communities, nations or broader areas, BEM is used for addressing the full breadth of issue areas and of people, animals/plants, and other natural resources. Here it helps identify what behaviors are associated with the relevant status indicators. It helps identify what ability and motivational factors are and would be determinants of improving status. The model determines what interventions could improve the motivation and ability factors and, as a result, improve status. Based on these, a strategy is being created for improving status for a whole person, community, country and world.

Person Model. The Person Model helps us to understand that each person goes through several life stages depending on how long they live. If status (e.g. health, income, performance) is to be improved, it is seldom a one-time intervention and generally should be done across the life span. As a result, the Person Model works by applying BEM over an individual person's time and life stages. (See Figure 4.3.)

The Person Model, with BEM as the underlying model, recognizes that each person is different at the beginning, throughout the life stages, and near the end. For status to be improved, the strategy needs to be both specific to each person across the life span and effective for all persons across the life span. (See Table 4.2.)

To date, the Person Model's primary use has been for improving health. Its potential use is being explored for creating an overall strategy for reducing vulnerability and improving the status of a person, community, country or broader area.

The model has been used to design the **HealthePeople** strategy to improve health and health care across America. The same design has applicability in a person, communities, states, and other countries. Its earliest use was in the middle 1970s to develop a high blood pressure control program in Milwaukee, Wisconsin. The desired behavior was adherence to a protocol for controlling high blood pressure over the person's remaining life. Through the use of the Person Model, the program was better able to understand how to match the intervention to time and different life stages. With respect to time, the interventions needed during the initial treatment were different than during the maintenance phase of treatment. With respect to life stages, interventions required refining for matching the behavioral determinants for a younger versus middle-age versus older persons. The blood pressure control program served as a model of community blood pressure control programs.

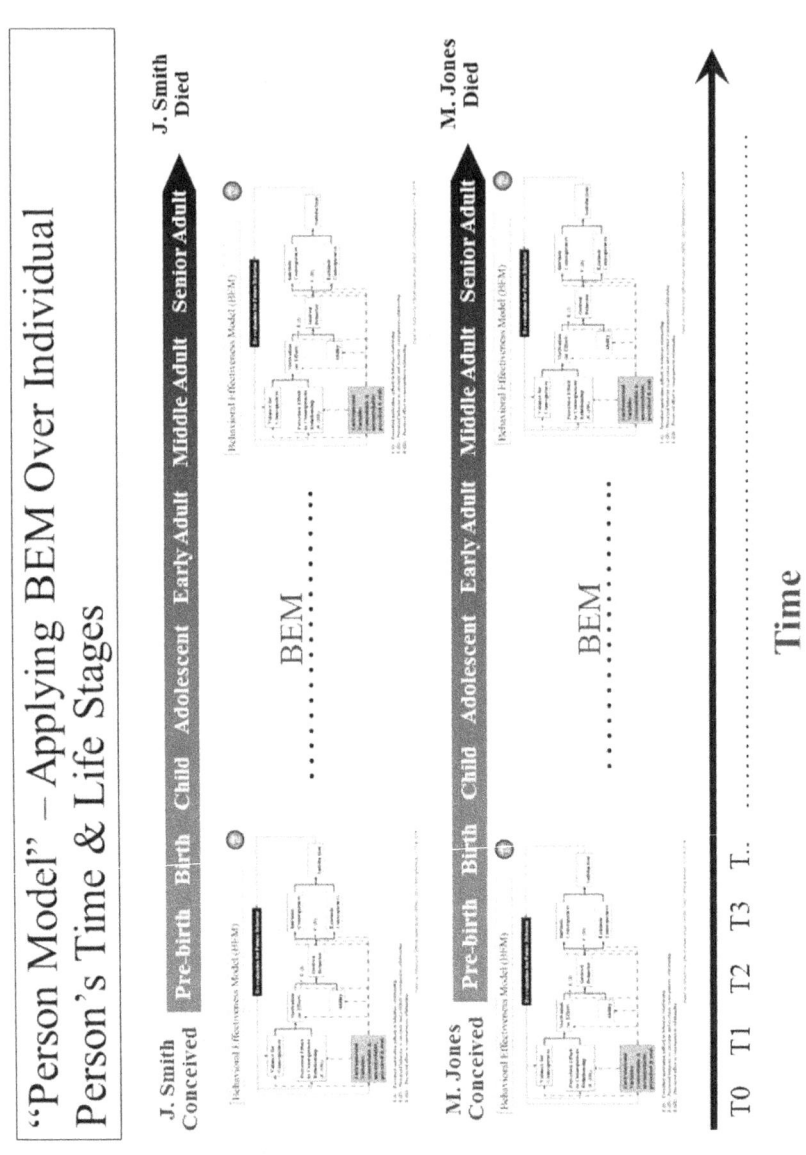

Figure 4.3. "Person Model" – Applying BEM Over Each Person's Time and Life Stages.

36

Table 4.2. Person Model – Applying BEM Over Each Person's Time and Life Stages

The Person Model use for achieving desired behavior is as follows:

1. Identify the person, persons or population whose behavior is targeted.
2. Decide what is the time frame or life stage(s) to be addressed. The preferred time frame is the whole life.
3. Decide what is the desired behavior or behaviors over time and through life stages.
4. Apply BEM as a recurring model (running the model as many times as necessary) adjusting to changes in motivation, ability and environmental variables.
5. Assess what interventions will best move projected behavior to desired behavior for the covered time and life stage(s).
6. Apply the interventions and assess their effect on an ongoing basis.
7. Adjust the interventions as needed over time and based on result.
8. Feed the interventions into the overall strategy and supporting strategies.

At the Centers for Medicare and Medicaid Services (CMS), the model was used in 2005 to enhance the overall strategy for national quality improvement for health care. The desired behavior was of health care providers over time and their careers. The model helped identify what target health care personnel behaviors, on an ongoing basis, could produce the best outcomes. Based on that, an approach was laid out using current and new interventions to improve health care provider behavior in a way that would produce improved outcomes and health status for the foreseeable future and over the health care providers' careers (life stages). These interventions were used to improve the overall quality improvement program for CMS.

The model was used in the early 2000s to create a new model called "person-centered health". (See Figure 4.4.) The Person-Centered Health Model has been used to refine the programs of the Veterans Health Administration, including overall care, care in the community and the VHA health information system (electronic health record and personal health record systems). It was also used at the Centers for Medicare and Medicaid Services to help with the draft strategic and operational plan.

The Person Model is also being used on the cross-cutting issue of vulnerability. Since vulnerability is relevant over a person's whole life span and changes through the life stages, the model helps identify what ability and motivational factors, over time and across life stages, would be determinants of vulnerability and thriving behavior. It recognizes that reducing vulnerability prior to birth is very different than doing so for an adolescent or for a senior adult. Some factors (e.g. financial and cognitive ability) carry across a person's life and can help lower vulnerability throughout a person's life. Some factors (e.g. ability reduced by Alzheimer's disease or low birth weight) always or most likely occur at a specific life stage. As a result, **Vulnerable In America and World**, the strategy for minimizing vulnerability and maximizing thriving in America and beyond, is a living strategy that adjusts for time and life stages. This comprehensive strategy has not been used to date, but is ready for application.

Population Model. The Population Model addresses status from the perspective of what is happening at any point in time and the effect on a diverse or non-diverse population. Again, BEM is the underlying model for adjusting strategy to address points in time across persons and their life stages. This model also applies to other differences (e.g., racial, ethnic, income, vulnerability) in the target population (See Figure 4.5.)

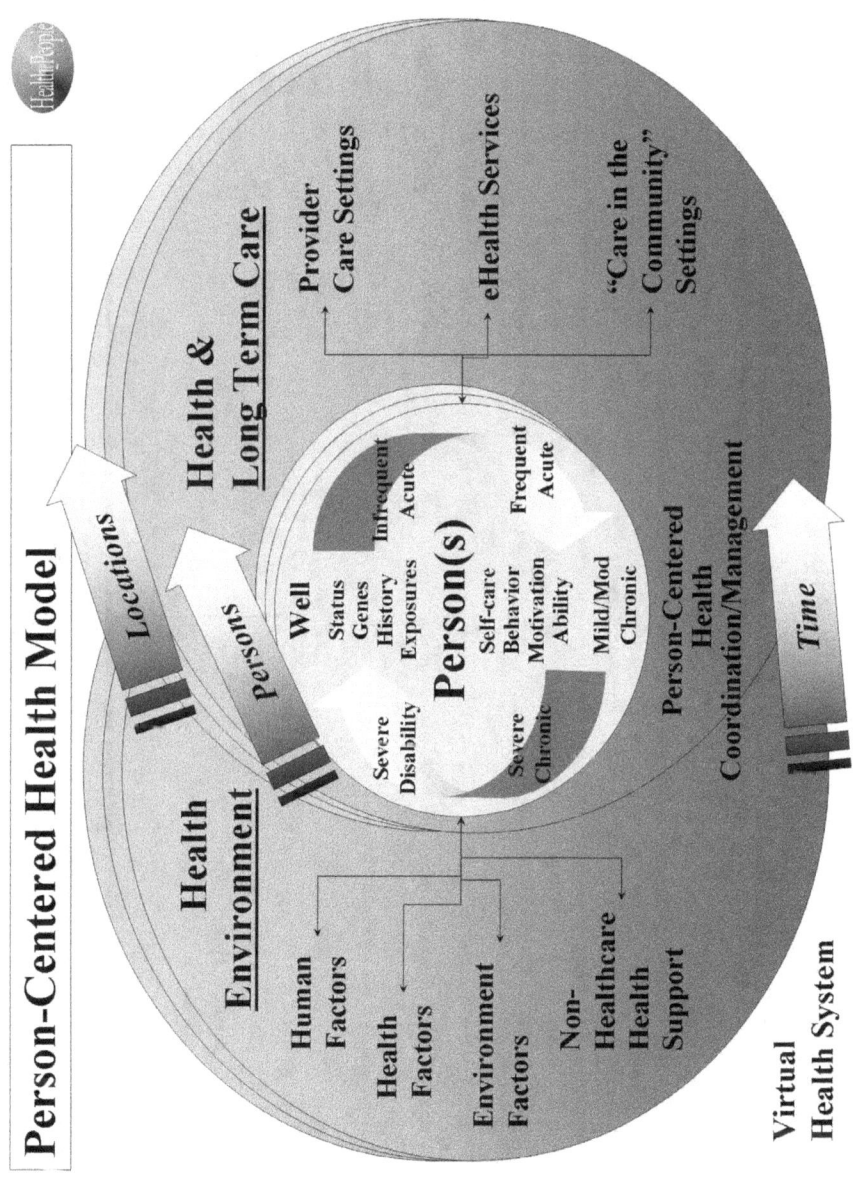

Figure 4.4. Person-Centered Health Model.

39

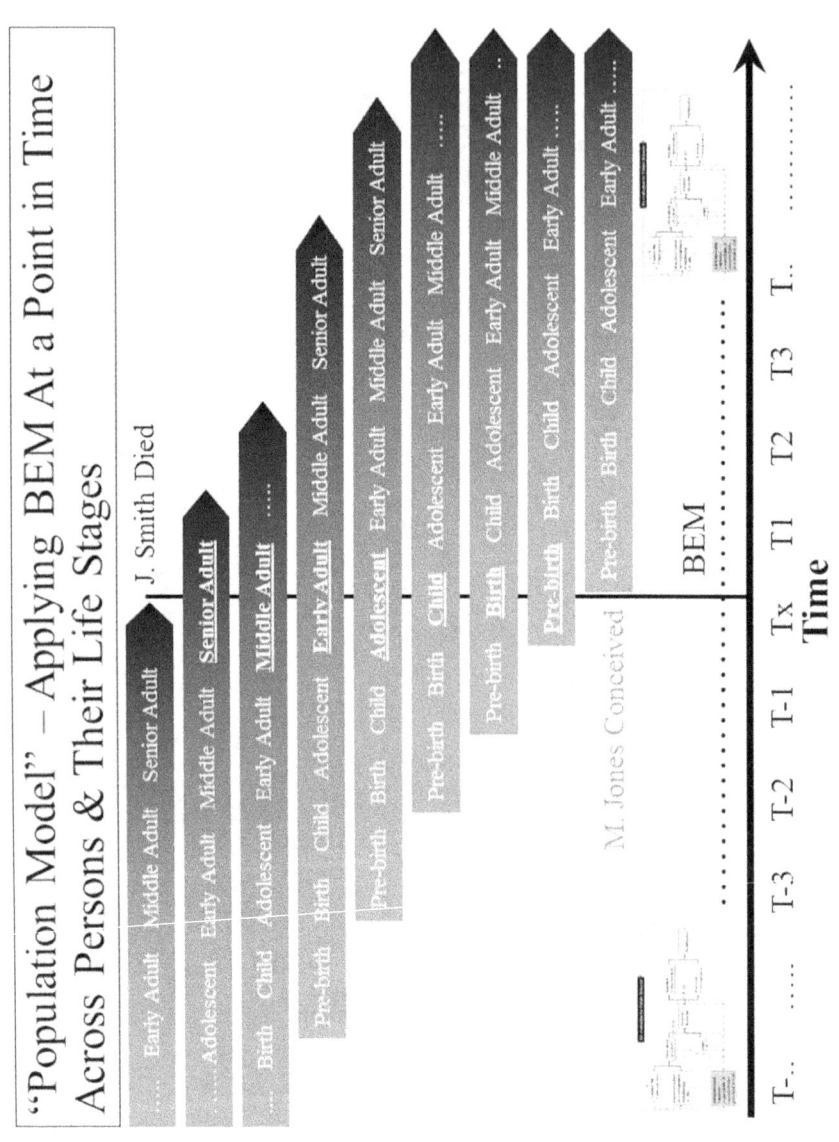

Figure 4.5. "Population Model" – Applying BEM at a Point in Time across Persons and Their Life Stages

The Population Model, with BEM as the underlying model, recognizes that strategy, at any point in time, must be both specific to each applicable person across the life span and effective across all persons across the life span. (See Table 4.3) Taking a time slice, the model recognizes that at any specific time, the target population likely includes persons from all different stages of life (pre-birth, birth, child, adolescent, early adult, middle adult and senior adult). At that time, each person has different status levels, different factors affecting status, and different responses to efforts at improving status. This can be seen in how major disasters (e.g., tsunamis, earthquakes, disease outbreaks, crop failures, and drought) affect people differently. This can be seen in how program interventions (e.g. education, housing programs, financial assistance, health insurance programs, heating assistance, taxes) affect people differently.

The Population Model's primary use to date has been for improving health. Its potential use is being explored for creating an overall strategy for reducing vulnerability and improving the status of a community, country or broader area.

At the Centers for Medicare and Medicaid Services (CMS), the model was used in 2006 to design the draft CMS Strategic and Operational Plan for 2007-12. It was used to address CMS's disparate beneficiary population and the timing and design of program interventions. The plan was designed to address the needs of both younger and older Medicaid beneficiaries, beneficiaries with disabilities, and healthier and severely ill Medicare beneficiaries. It also addressed the populations that are pre-Medicaid and pre-Medicare. The plan recognized that over time, these populations change as new age cohorts moved into the program. These Population Model interventions were then used to develop the draft overall Strategic and Operational Plan for CMS.

41

Table 4.3. Population Model – Applying BEM at a Point in Time across Persons and Their Life Stages

The Population Model use for achieving desired behavior is as follows:

1. Identify the population whose behavior is targeted.
2. Decide what are the point(s) in time and life stage(s) to be addressed.
3. Decide what is the desired behavior or behaviors at different points in time across persons and their life stages.
4. Apply the BEM model across time and across populations and their life stages taking into account their differing motivation, ability and environmental variables.
5. Assess what interventions will best move projected behavior to desired behavior across time and across populations and their life stages.
6. Apply the interventions and assess their effect on a population on an ongoing basis.
7. Adjust the interventions as needed over time and based on result.
8. Feed the interventions into the overall strategy and supporting strategies.

For the DoD Military Health System (MHS), the model was used in the 1990s to work with pre-military, active service, Guard and Reserve, veterans, retirees and their families. All are the responsibility of the MHS. Key points in time greatly affect how the health programs work and their effect. Earlier wars (and their effects) such as the two World Wars and the Korean War are very different than the Vietnam War than the first Iraq War, as well as the second Iraq War and then the Afghanistan operations. They are all likely to be different than future wars and other military actions. All of these factors were built into the overall strategy for the future Military Health System that was re-engineered to improve performance, adopted as a force health protection program, and was made more flexible to adjust to different futures.

The model has also been used to design a **Health₂People** strategy to improve health and health care across America. The same design has applicability in communities, states, and other countries.

The Population Model is also being used on the cross-cutting issue of vulnerability. Since vulnerability is relevant at different points across a person's life stages, it is used to help identify what ability and motivational factors at those different points are most likely determinants of vulnerability and thriving behavior. For example, applying new policies on financial assistance or taxes over the next twelve months will have very different effects across the population of persons. If the intent of the new policies is reducing financial vulnerability and/or increasing overall thriving across the U.S. population, then they must be modeled, at a minimum, against each subpopulation and, preferably, against each "person". The more desirable policies are those that both reduce vulnerability most for the most vulnerable and substantially reduce vulnerability for all persons. The most desirable policies are the ones that do this and continue the positive effect as the population moves through time (i.e., sustainable, reduced vulnerability for all people). As indicated earlier, the overall strategy has not been used to date, but is ready for application.

5. Building Thriving Future Using Behavior Effectiveness Model (BEM)

Most recently, the Behavior Effectiveness Model (BEM) and related models have been used to build *Thrive!®* – a vision, strategy, model and tools for building, achieving and sustaining a surviving and thriving future for all forever. Achieving a thriving future depends on human behavior. Achieving a thriving future depends on a successful change effort for human behavior which the author calls the **Thrive! Endeavor®** (TE).

What the **Thrive! Endeavor** and this human behavior need to achieve is a thriving future where you, your community, your country and our world are thriving:

- performing well,
- being well-off (financially),
- being well nourished,
- being well housed,
- being well protected (exposures, crime),
- being well educated,
- being physically and mentally well (people),
- growing/developing well,
- living within good habitat,
- being physically well (Earth, plants, animals, environment),
- not being vulnerable,
- producing personal and public goods,
- living within a stable, positive climate, and
- being sustained.

Why must you and we care about a surviving and thriving future for you and your friends and family, your community, your country and our world? You and all of us want and need that future because of our endangered future and our human need to survive and desire to thrive. What drives us (motivation) is that a person and a people need to survive and desire to thrive in the current world and a sustainable future world.

To truly satisfy this need and desire, we need (motivation) the following:

1) we, as a person and a people, need to survive and desire to thrive,

2) we depend on other persons for survival and thriving, especially in the long term,

3) our need and desire applies to both the current and future world,

4) our future survival and thriving depends on there being a future world, and

5) our future world must be sustainable and sustained to fully meet our need and desire.

Achieving a surviving and thriving future is dependent on these being the primary drivers of and motivation for future human behavior. Helping to make that happen is the rationale and role for BEM and the **Thrive! Endeavor**.

The **Thrive! Endeavor**.works with people who have both the motivation and ability to create and sustain positive, large and timely change. It helps build and execute strategy that will build a thriving future for you, your community, your country or our world. Table 5.1 lays out the strategy building steps.

See accompanying book – **Thrive! – Building a Thriving Future** (www.ThriveEndeavor.org) for details on the following steps and models:

- Systems Model (including "Ideal Systems"),
- Status Model,

- via Model,
- Status Model,
- Performance Improvement Model, and
- Strategy and Supportive Strategies Model.

Though the strategy building steps in Table 5.1 imply sequential application that is not always the case. Step 1 is important in our understanding the current system (you, community, country or world), its status, its projected actions, and its projected people and population behaviors. Step 1c helps us organize that thinking of how we might get from the current situation to a better and thriving future for the targeted system (you, community, country or world). Step 2 helps us work through what needs to be changed and how we might make that change. Step 3 pulls all this together to help us create and execute the overall strategy and supportive strategies. Step 4 is to make sure we evaluate how we are doing and provide input for changes in strategy. Step 5 focuses on the successful execution of the overall strategy and supportive strategies. Step 6 makes sure we understand that strategy is not static and needs to adjust to unanticipated input and environmental changes, and the strategy needs to be executed successfully on an ongoing basis.

Table 5.1. Overall Strategy for Creating and Sustaining Positive, Large Scale Change and Building Thriving Future

The overall strategy is as follows:
1. Assess current and projected state of target person, community, country or world.
    a. Use Systems Model (including "Ideal Systems") to understand targeted person, community, country or world today.
    b. Use Status Model to identify current status for "whole" person, community, country or world targeted for positive, large scale change.

---

    c. Use via Model to analyze the positive/negative actions currently impacting or projected to impact "whole" person, community, country or world.

    d. Use Person Model to identify what individual people are likely to do in future.

    e. Use Population Model to identify what populations are likely to do in future.

    f. Use Behavioral Effectiveness Model (BEM) to assess projected people behaviors.

2. Design strategy to achieve desired status for"whole" person, community, country or world.

    a. Use Systems Model (incl. "Ideal Systems") to identify desired future system state.

    b. Use Status Model to identify desired status for targeted system.

    c. Use Performance Improvement Model to identify changes, including behavior, needed to progress from current status and achieve desired status for targeted system.

    d. Use via Model to identify potential interventions for creating and sustaining desired positive, large scale change.

    e. Use Person Model to identify what individual people should do to help achieve the desired positive, large scale change.

    f. Use Population Model to identify what populations of people should do to help achieve the desired positive, large scale change.

    g. Use BEM to identify ability, motivation and desired behaviors that help achieve desired change and to develop supportive strategies to achieve desired behaviors.

    h. Use Strategy and Supportive Strategies Model to identify and assess and organize supportive strategies (sets of interventions) for creating/sustaining desired change.

3. With above inputs, develop overall, self-perpetuating strategy for creating and sustaining desired positive, large scale change across target person, community, country or world.

4. Apply evaluation methodology for assessing strategies' and interventions' impact on near and long term status and for implications for future interventions and strategies.

5. Execute overall strategy and supportive strategies successfully.

6. Adjust and execute overall strategy and supportive strategies to meet changing inputs and environment.

To assess current and projected behaviors for the persons who need and want a better future, we use BEM (See Figure 5.1) as follows:

- Identify the persons (the person, the community, the country, our world) who need and want a better future.

- Decide what behaviors are key to a better future. Note that some behavior is one-time and some is recurring.

- Assess motivation in terms of its current and future characteristics.

- Assess ability in terms of its current and future characteristics.

- Assess environmental variables, both controllable and uncontrollable and both perceived and real.

- Assess how motivation, ability and environmental variables are likely to affect future behavior without further intervention.

- Assess what are likely to be the intrinsic (internal to person(s)) and extrinsic (external to person(s)) consequences of projected behavior and what is likely to be the person's or persons' satisfaction.

- Assess how consequences and satisfaction are likely to affect future behavior
- Assess how projected behavior, without further intervention, matches to behavior needed to build and achieve a better future.

To identify how a person(s) is likely to behave without and then with the **Thrive! Endeavor**, we use the **Person Model** to the extent feasible. This is important because persons may behave in very different ways over time. We get closer to identifying and understanding a person's or persons' behavior to the extent we successfully:

- Identify the person(s) whose behavior is targeted.
- Determine the time frame or life stage(s) to be addressed. The preferred time frame is the person's or persons' whole life.
- Apply the Behavioral Effectiveness Model (BEM) across time and across the person(s) and his/her life stages taking into account differing motivation, ability, behavior, and environmental variables.
- Determine the likely behavior(s) over time and through life stages.

The power to make large, positive, and timely change is greatest when we apply our efforts to a person(s) desired or needed change and when a person(s) want to make that positive change.

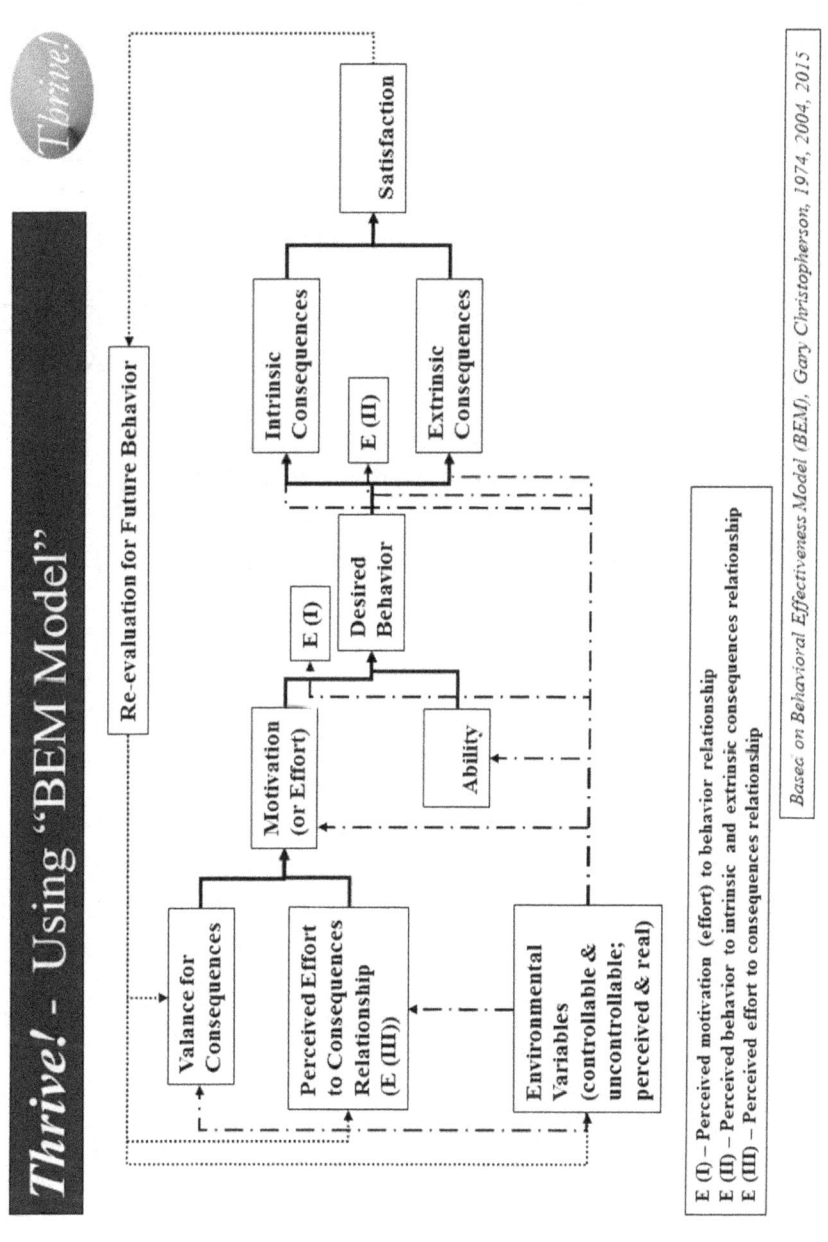

Figure 5.1. Thrive! – Using BEM Model

Similar to the **Person Model**, we use the **Population Model** to identify what the community's, the country's or the world's whole population or subpopulations are likely to do without and then with the **Thrive! Endeavor**. This step plays an especially important role when we lack information at the individual person level and/or when an intervention can't be customized at the individual person level. We get closer to identifying and understanding population behavior to the extent we successfully:

- Identify the population whose behavior is targeted.
- Decide what the point(s) are in time and life stage(s) to be addressed.
- Apply the BEM model across time and across subpopulations and their life stages taking into account differing motivation, ability and environmental variables.
- Determine the likely behavior(s) over time and through life stages.

Each and all of us should develop and do as many positive behaviors (decisions and/or actions) as we can. The more positive behaviors, the better for all of us. Each and all of us should do behaviors that help build, achieve and sustain a surviving and thriving future for ourselves. Each and all of us should do behaviors that help build, achieve and sustain a surviving and thriving future for our community. Each and all of us should do behaviors that help build, achieve and sustain a surviving and thriving future for our country. Each and all of us should do behaviors that help build, achieve and sustain a surviving and thriving future for our world, including the Earth on which we depend.

What positive behaviors are needed to bring about the needed changes that improve our current status enough to achieve the desired surviving and thriving status? (See Figure 5.2) Each and all of us must do behaviors that support good changes that will help reduce vulnerability and/or improve and/or sustain surviving and thriving. If good changes are likely to occur, together we support them. If good changes are not likely to occur, together we support them and develop other good changes to compensate.

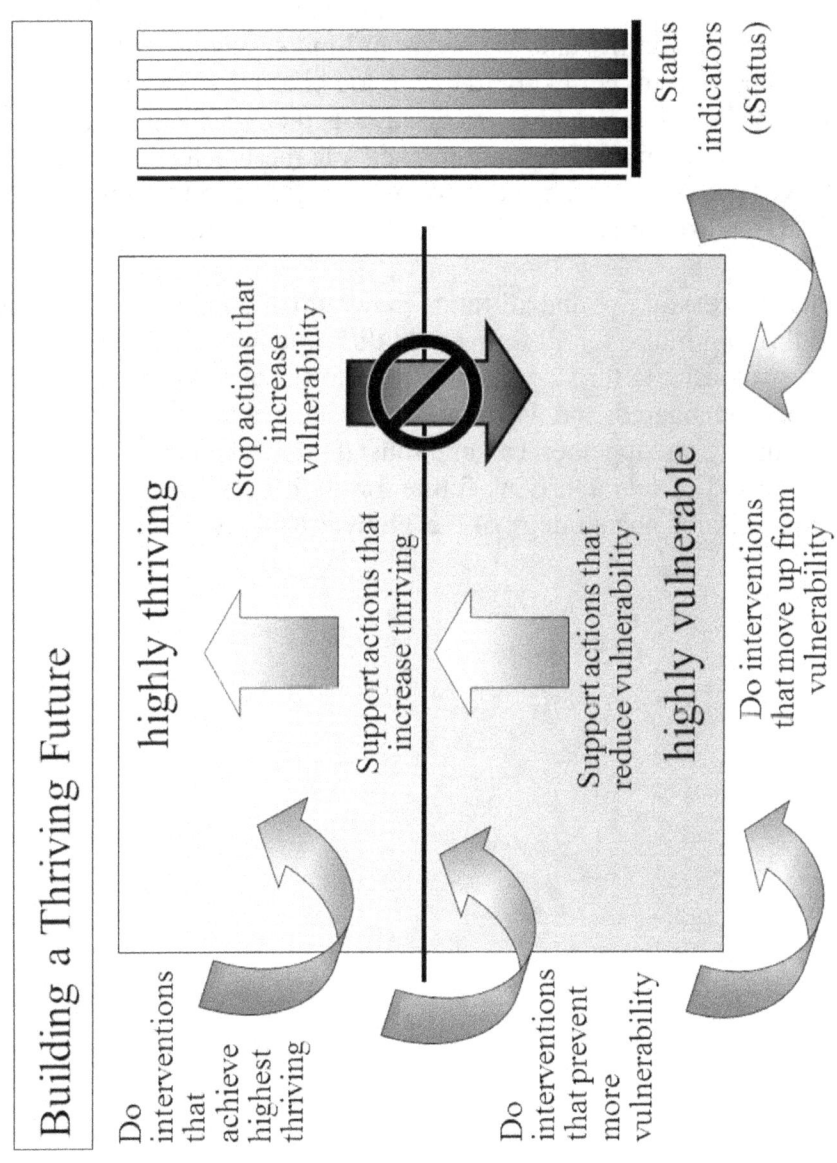

Figure 5.2. Building a Thriving Future

53

Each and all of us must do behaviors that stop <u>bad</u> changes that increase vulnerability and/or prevent or limit surviving and thriving. If bad changes are not likely to occur, together we ensure they do not. If bad changes are likely to occur, together we change them, stop them or avoid/reduce their impact. Via these behaviors and the **Thrive! Endeavor**, <u>each and all of us together</u> can and should build, achieve and sustain a surviving and thriving future for all forever.

When successful, we and all future generations achieve the surviving and thriving future for all forever. At this time in human history when we desire to thrive, when we need to survive, when our future is most endangered, and when we are most capable, all of us individually and together, can and must do the behaviors that build, achieve and sustain a thriving future for all forever. That is the vision, mission and strategy of the **Thrive! Endeavor**.

Brief Bibliography

Campbell, J.P., M.D. Dunnette, E.E. Lawler, and K.E. Weick, Managerial Behavior, Performance, and Effectiveness, McGraw-Hill, 1970.

Christopherson, G.A., People Planning: Increasing Planning Effectiveness by Working with User and Implementer Behavior, Master's Thesis, University of Wisconsin (Madison), 1974.

Cummings, L.L., Lectures on Organizational Behavior and Human Performance, University of Wisconsin (Madison) School of Business, 1973.

Cummings, L.L., and D.P.Schwab, Performance in Organizations: Determinants and Appraisal, Scott-Foresman, Inc. 1973.

Galbraith, J. and L.L. Cummings, "An Empirical Investigation of the Motivational Determinants of Task Performance: Interactive Effects Between Instrumentality-Valence and Motivation-Ability", Organizational Behavior and Human Performance, Vol. 2 (1967), pp. 237-57.

Goodman, P.S., Antecedent Factors Affecting Valences, Instrumentalities, and Expectancies, Carnegie-Mellon University, August, 1973.

House, R.J., "A Path Goal Theory of Leader Effectiveness", Administrative Science Quarterly, 16 (1971), pp 321-38.

House, R.J., H.J. Shapiro, and M.A. Wahba, "Expectancy Theory as a Predictor of Work Behavior and Attitude: A Re-evaluation of Empirical Evidence", Working Paper, September, 1973.

Lawler, E.E., Pay and Organizational Effectiveness, McGraw-Hill, 1971.

Porter, L.W., and E.E. Lawler, Managerial Attitudes and Performance, Irwing-Dorsey, 1968.

Vroom, V., Work and Motivation, John Wiley & Sons, 1964.